Growing
Old
In
America

Growing Old In America

Elaine Landau

Julian Messner  New York

JULIAN MESSNER and colophon are trademarks of Simon & Schuster, Inc.

10 9 8 7 6 5 4 3 2 1

Manufactured in the United States of America

Design by Teresa Delgado, A Good Thing Inc.

Library of Congress Cataloging in Publication Data

Landau, Elaine.
  Growing old in America.

  Bibliography: p.
  Includes index.
  Summary: Discusses aspects of growing old in America, such as retirement, senior citizen centers and communities, financial matters, and health problems.
    1. Aged—United States—Juvenile literature.
  2. Retirement—United States—Juvenile literature.
  [1. Old age. 2. Retirement] I. Title.
  HQ1064.U5L297 1985   305.2'6'0973   84-27244
  ISBN 0-671-42409-2

For Irving Pearl—
A Very Special Person At Any Age!

Contents

Growing
Old
In
America

Becoming Old

OLD AGE. FOR many people those words still conjure up an image of elderly individuals wasting away in nursing homes or perhaps living in shabby tenements, existing on canned dog food and day-old bread. Old has become synonymous with exhaustion, helplessness, and dependency. Advancing years seemingly rob us of beauty, vitality, and value to society, yet the aging process is one aspect of living that is inescapable. It cannot be stopped; everyone eventually grows old.

Most people dread the loss of youth, but how accurate are the negative stereotypes that have come to characterize aging? Is everyone past sixty sick, infirm, leading a life of misery? Who is "old" today, anyway?

When perceived in the overall view, growing old in America presents a diversified picture. Gerontology, a relatively new addition to the social sciences, is a discipline that encompasses all aspects of aging and provides an insight to the changes that may occur in people after they pass middle age. Currently, gerontologists divide older people into two distinct groups. Where old age was once referred to uniformly as one phase of life, gerontologists have separated aging adults into categories of the young-old (sixty-five to seventy-five) and the old-old (seventy-five and older).

But even these cut-off dates are not rigidly observed. Some gerontologists will designate people about fifty-five years of age who may have elected to retire early as young-olds and apply the same label to some individuals over seventy-five who clearly demonstrate the traits characteristic of the younger group. The general lowering of our society's retirement age now makes fifty-five meaningful for the young-old. Many workers look forward to such early retirement, and they follow through with their plans when they feel that they can exist comfortably on retirement incomes. In certain industries where overall employment is declining, the downward spiral of the workers' retirement age is even more dramatic, and many experts predict that the trend will continue, thus making the young-old group an increasingly large portion of America's retired population.

Older people, of course, are still people, each one an individual in his or her own right. The following statistics, however, may help to illuminate their lifestyle as a group.

A. Approximately one out of every ten people living in the United States today is over sixty-five years of age. In 1973 the life expectancy for a male was 67.6 years and for a female, 75.3 years, while a baby boy born in 1900 could expect to live forty-six years and a baby girl forty-eight years. These additional years of life expectancy were achieved not through control of the aging process, but by improved sanitation and the conquest of major childhood diseases which often proved fatal. A woman of sixty-five today can expect to live another 17.5 years, and a man of that age may currently hope to extend his life an additional 13.4 years.

B. According to the United States Census Bureau, the sixty-five-and-over population is on the rise, comprising an estimated 215.1 million people. If the relatively low birth rate and declining death rate remain at their present levels, elderly citizens will account for approximately 17 percent of the U.S. population—one out of every six Americans—by the year 2050.

C. Contrary to what is believed to be true, only a small percentage (about 5 percent) of older Americans reside in nursing homes and over 80 percent of these individuals are over seventy-five years of age. If only 5 percent of the elderly live in nursing homes, obviously 95 percent still function in the outside world.

The young-old are a relatively healthy group, with fewer than one out of four limiting any of their major activities due to health. Although there is a number of widows, the intact couple is most common, the majority of them living in their own households.

D. Another prevalent myth is that "old folks" are kept at home alone, left behind and forgotten by their children. Studies indicate that more than 80 percent of such people over sixty-five see their children at least once every two weeks.

Most sons and daughters still make their own homes fairly close to the homes of their parents, though it is difficult to evaluate the quality of these frequent contacts. Is it a sense of familial obligation or a deep, loving affection that draws individuals of diverse ages together? Each instance may have its own explanation. Often such relationships extend to grandchildren and even great grandchildren, spanning two or more generations.

E. Senior citizens often see themselves in a perspective that is different from that of the general public. A recent survey by pollster Louis Harris revealed that people over sixty-five have a much higher sense of self-esteem than society usually attribues to them. Among the general public, 21 percent indicated that they regarded the elderly as useful, functioning members of the community. When the same question was asked of older people, 40 percent responded affirmatively about their position as vital members of society.

F. People over sixty-five years of age are still romantically and sexually active. Statistics on marriage gleaned from the federal government show that older adults, who have divorced or lost a spouse, do remarry. Some older couples may even reside together without the benefit of marriage because a legal union would lessen the amount of social security income they receive as singles. Still, in 1975, over 17 million women over sixty-five years of age were married. More than 32 million men over sixty-five years of age were married as well.

G. An extensive study sponsored by the National Council on the Aging exposed many false notions that still persist regarding the elderly, such as the most common of these, that senility is inevitably linked with aging. A minority of older people do become senile, but the reasons vary and often have nothing to do with age. The cause of senility may be genetically linked, due to disease factors, or perhaps even due to diet. Some individuals who may exhibit signs of mental illness in their old age may have actually suffered from varying mental disturbances throughout their lives.

Although a breakdown need not be anticipated with the onset of old age, certain mental capacities tend to diminish. For example, older people may find it more difficult to recall new facts or events than to remember the more distant past. Yet, this tendency may often become exaggerated due to unfair stereotyping. If a young or middle-aged woman misplaces her car keys when she changes handbags, it's accepted without much comment. But if an older woman does the same thing, people shrug their shoulders and say her memory is going. Unfortunately, in many instances, the older woman will begin to doubt herself and her own abilities and tend to agree with the critics, thus adding strength to their argument.

Age and aging may cause difficulties for people at all stages of life and for society as a whole. Many of these problems, however, are social, not biological, in nature. Some difficulties arise from a phenomenon known as age stratification, wherein individuals and the roles or tasks they perform are sharply defined according to age. When people with essentially the same feelings and potential are so distinctly (yet artificially) segregated, a certain amount of inequality and eventually conflict may erupt. If people are categorized as young, middle-aged, and old without regard to individual abilities, the inequality may result when those in one strata have restricted access to valued roles and the rewards such roles bring. For

example, teenagers and people over sixty-five are often denied high-level employment opportunities.

Segregating age groups is pervasive in our social institutions. This limits the opportunities people have to form a relationship with someone of a different generation. Even grade-school children are discouraged from interacting with children older or younger than themselves. Older people living in retirement communities or nursing homes generally have little or no contact with younger people. When society imposes this type of unnatural segregation on people, opportunities for an exchange of support and influence between people of different ages are shut off.

Today many gerontologists think it crucial that our society move toward an ideal in which arbitrary age constraints are removed, and all individuals are offered opportunities in accordance with their needs, desires, and abilities. We cannot afford to view an older person as first being old and then being a person. He or she is simply a person who happens to be old. Aging is a cultural process as well as a personal and physiological one. It is important not to treat older people as a problem, but to regard them as a resource.

Today the young-old group is carving out new service roles to enhance communities. Literally millions of older people who have refused to lead desperate lives of quiet solitude have banded together at local, state, and national levels to form influential organizations that work effectively for their needs. Within the past two decades, over three hundred national organizations have arisen to deal with the problems facing the elderly.

It is conceivable that the groundwork now laid may become a major force of social change that will advance our society toward a time when a person's age will be considered irrelevant. Older Americans who can create an attractive image of aging will help to eradicate negative stereotypes and meaningless age norms.

There are countless cases of individuals over sixty-five who have created new, exciting, and stimulating lives for themselves. Marian M. is one such person. When Marian was a college student, she majored in languages, specializing in Spanish and French. She also developed a strong liking for foreign things during this period. She never missed an international festival, and tried to see all of the few foreign films that were shown in her small New Jersey hometown.

Marian had always wanted to visit the places she had read about and seen on the screen, but during her college years there was little time or money for travel. Marian, whose mother had died when she was fifteen, was the oldest in a family of five children. Marian's father did not remarry, and since he spent most of his time working at two jobs to support the family, the role of housekeeper and mother fell largely to Marian. While still a student, Marian lived at home where she shopped, cooked, and cleaned the house for her family between attending classes and doing homework.

In her senior year of college, Marian became engaged to Douglas, an engineering student she met on campus. She married him shortly after her graduation that June. Although Marian had dreamed of a honeymoon tour through Europe, the young couple could only afford a short weekend trip to Niagara Falls.

Douglas went on to graduate school in engineering in the fall, while Marian found work teaching languages in the local high school. This provided a measure of support while Douglas continued his studies. Although Marian did not earn a great deal of money, she loved her work.

While she was teaching, Marian had hoped to travel to Europe during her summer vacations with her husband, but the couple never seemed to have enough money to make the trip. Time passed. Finally, after more than twenty years of teaching foreign languages, Marian and Douglas were able to take their first trip to Europe. The trip proved to be everything Marian had hoped it would be. Upon returning home, Douglas told all of their friends that he had become a travel addict, and vowed that he and Marian would return to Europe the following summer.

Unfortunately, things did not turn out as the couple had hoped. Douglas had a fatal heart attack and died that winter. As she had previously planned, Marian retired from her teaching job the following June.

By now, Marian's children had all grown up and were leading separate lives. Suddenly, Marian realized that after being so vitally needed by so many people for so many years, she was now alone. Marian didn't relish her predicament, and the worst aspect was that for the first time she felt she had no goal or purpose.

At first, Marian became depressed. She felt she might spend the last years of her life watching television, crocheting, and occasionally visiting her grandchildren. Then Marian decided to rescue herself. At sixty-five years of age, she embarked on a new venture—that of becoming a world traveler. Marian found her new freedom exhilarating. Marian climbed up steep, rocky cliffs, bartered with peddlers in bazaars and marketplaces, and sampled exotic foods. At times Marian has taken her children and some of her older grandchildren along with her on her trips.

As Marian expressed her feelings:

I may not be able to leave my children and grandchildren a lot of money when I die, but I will have left them some things that are rare and precious. Beth will remember the trip to Mexico with her grandmother for the rest of her life. My younger grandchildren have received postcards of colorful places from many different continents. They've been both delighted and enchanted by bedtime tales of how children live in other lands. My experiences have been educational as well as exciting for them.

But perhaps the most important thing I have to leave my heirs is the example my lifestyle has set for them. I was not a grandmother who spent the later years of her life knitting baby booties in a wooden rocking chair. Through my experience, both my children and my grandchildren have learned that it's never too late to add a new dimension to your life. Life does not end at sixty-five, and there is no reason to pass up exciting possibilities, just because you have already lived for a certain number of years. I want my family to know that a person is able to experience and grow at any age. You are not automatically too old to try something new just because society dictates that a given activity is inappropriate for someone of your age. Showing the people I love that you don't necessarily have to live out the last years of your life waiting for death is the greatest gift I can leave them.

Steven F. is an eighty-six-year-old retired dentist who lives in a New York City nursing home. While a young man, Steven led what might be considered a dashing life. His ample income allowed him to have a large, luxurious New York City apartment, a small cattle ranch in Texas, and frequent gambling excursions to the Caribbean.

A number of Steven's friends and family members were quite critical of his lifestyle. It was continually suggested to Steven that he should settle down, marry, and raise a family. Steven's brother stressed to Steven that although living as a carefree bachelor might be fine for a short time, he would regret it as he grew older.

Steven, however, had no intention of changing his personal life. "When I grow older I don't expect to undergo some miraculous personality transformation. I've always enjoyed freedom and diversification, and I suspect I still will thirty or forty years from now."

When Steven became too ill to live by himself any longer, he entered a nursing home. Although well into his eighties, Steven was still quite a gregarious fellow, and he made friends easily in his new surroundings.

Even after he had suffered a stroke and was confined to a wheelchair, he continued to date the resident ladies at the nursing home.

Steven had enjoyed his youth and continued to enjoy life in his old age.

Today, Steven is still at the same nursing home. Whenever anyone remarks how terrible it must be to be old, he reminds that individual that the essence of fulfillment is not connected with the number of years one lives but in one's approach to life.

Retirement: An Ending or a New Beginning?

RETIREMENT REPRESENTS A monumental turning point in an individual's life and there's no established script for the retirement role. How a person will spend the oncoming years after leaving a job will depend more on his or her own resourcefulness than on any socially structured situation. In short, retirement represents a new phase that always involves a challenge.

Two seemingly contradictory trends regarding retirement appear to be evident currently in the United States. There is a movement by many people who want to continue working to do away with mandatory or forced retirement. At the same time, many others are beginning to press for early retirement, and their number is increasing.

There are many personal choices involved regarding retirement. It's important to explore all the ramifications.

In 1978 a major change in age-related retirement practices resulted from the passage of federal legislation. This raised the minimum mandatory retirement age from sixty-five to seventy in most private industries and also eliminated age restrictions altogether for nearly all federal employees as of January 1, 1979.

The law does not force any worker to remain on the job until age seventy; it simply makes the decision a matter of personal choice. There are two major exceptions. Some very well-paid executives in certain specified positions may still be made to retire at sixty-five. Workers engaged in high-risk occupations, such as police officers or fire fighters, may be subject to forced retirement when it can be clearly demonstrated that their age is a legitimate factor in job performance.

A study by the Department of Labor has shown that doing away with mandatory retirement will only increase the size of the labor force about one-half of one percent. Ironically, this is because most older workers would voluntarily choose to retire at about sixty-five. In 1977, when the Connecticut General Life Insurance Company abolished mandatory retirement for its employees at age sixty-five, less than 5 percent elected to continue at their jobs. Nevertheless, many employees feel it is important that the choice be theirs.

The trend toward early retirement actually began in the early 1960s and gained momentum when the social security pay-out age, with reduced benefits, was lowered to sixty-two. Since that time, it has become common practice for companies like Sears and General Motors to offer pensions with a bonus for early retirement to both professional and nonprofessional employees. Where such liberal pension plans are in effect, employees are retiring at fifty-five or even in their late forties. The federal government offers a pension with a built-in cost-of-living adjustment.

What type of person chooses to retire early? A study conducted by the University of Michigan Survey Research Center revealed that early retirees generally feel that they will have an adequate income for their needs, inasmuch as their family responsibilities are diminishing at this point in their lives. Some of these people may experience dissatisfaction with their work or are under strong pressure from family members or friends to leave their jobs. A number of the individuals interviewed stated that they were looking forward to new travel and recreational activities they could enjoy while they were still in relatively good health.

A wide range of services are available to help workers prepare for retirement, offering information and sometimes instruction on financial management, legal problems, government services, health care, and housing, to name but a few. Corporations, labor unions, and professional societies often offer educational seminars. There's written material on various aspects of retirement planning published by associations of retired people, insurance companies, and local mental health associations, as well as a growing number of general books and articles on the subject.

One way people can help prepare themselves for retirement is through guidance counseling sessions now offered by about 25 percent of the corporations in the United States. An individual who may have associated his personal identity with his work may feel a loss of purpose and prestige when his employment comes to an end. The problem of feeling rejected and of suffering from a sense of worthlessness can be just as real as the financial pressures that retirement may bring.

Retirement may necessitate adjustments within the individual's home life as well. Husbands and wives may have different ideas about how they wish to spend their retirement. Where one spouse may want to remain in the same surroundings and continue life as it was, the other may yearn to travel, move, or embark on a new lifestyle.

In addition, many couples are not prepared to face a future of unrelenting togetherness. Husbands and wives who were separated for hours each day while working may now find themselves spending considerable time together. This is not always desirable. In more than one instance, retirement has jolted a peaceful ongoing relationship.

Many corporations now offer professional counseling services to their employees approaching retirement. In guidance sessions dealing with retirement, potential conflicts like this are handled. Many seminars encourage attendance by both spouses. The sessions can also help the retiree anticipate decisions that will have to be made on issues and preferences not previously considered. Does the retiree want to remain in his or her present home or move? If he moves, will he be able to locate suitable housing at a price he can afford? Will the retiree be better off in a large urban community or a small town or village?

Does the retiree value privacy more than interaction with contemporaries?

All of these decisions are highly personal. There are no right or wrong answers. Each retiree must consider what is right for him.

Besides the guidance counseling seminars offered by various corporations, a number of specialized retirement counseling services have evolved. One of the better known among them is Retirement Advisors, Inc. (RAI). It has existed for over twenty years, developing retirement programs primarily suited to executives, union employees, and other specialized groups.

RAI sells its services to an interested company, rather than to individuals. It offers a full range of assistance that includes developing group counseling programs, providing speakers, and initiating follow-up services to recently retired employees.

Many retirement experts agree that if pre-retirement programs are to be effective, they can't be initiated a month or two before the worker is scheduled to retire. Action for Independent Maturity (AIM), a division of the American Association of Retired Persons (AARP), recruits its members from the ranks of workers who range in age from about fifty-five to sixty-five and who are still actively engaged in their careers. AIM offers planning seminars and publications to help the employee consider the various phases of retirement ahead of time. Unlike RAI, individuals join AIM on their own. Some corporations, unions, and retirement organizations will encourage serious consideration about retirement twenty or thirty years beforehand.

Perhaps one of the cruelest myths in our society today is that productive life ends when you retire from your nine-to-five job. Not so. One option is to embark on a second career, as Iris and Steve Brennan chose to do. Steve, a registered pharmacist, had owned a drugstore, which he sold when he retired. Iris had spent the past twenty-seven years working as a physical therapist in a large urban hospital.

Soon after they retired, the Brennans elected to abandon city life. They moved to upstate New York where they purchased a large fruit orchard. Initially, Steve and Iris had not intended to go into business for themselves. When their orchard yielded far more produce than they themselves could eat or give away, however, the couple set up a fruit and apple cider stand. Their small business thrived. They soon gained marketing expertise by reading everything available on the subject, as well as by seeking out

advice from those knowledgeable in the field, and in time the tiny enterprise grew into a successful gourmet food and gift store.

Not everyone has the capital or aptitude to establish a small business of his own, but numerous second career opportunities are beginning to present themselves for senior citizens. A growing number of professional positions involve services for the elderly, such as directors of senior centers, counselors, and administrators at nursing homes. Many of these full-time positions are now second careers for people past fifty-five.

Another option after retirement is part-time work. Partial employment is ideal for retired people who can use some extra money, but do not need a full-time salary. Some retirees want a job that is not too physically tiring, but insist they need enough work to keep them from feeling cut off from the mainstream of activity. Part-time employment situations take numerous forms—a few hours work each weekday, full days but fewer days per week, flexible hours, and shared jobs.

It is not always easy for older people to return to work. They sometimes experience difficulty in finding jobs. Most of the private and state employment services in the United States are not equipped to deal with large numbers of elderly people seeking employment. The term "older worker" often applies to anyone over forty, and many employment agencies are not interested in handling part-time positions.

In recent years, a new type of service has appeared that promises hope for capable elderly people who still wish to work. Senior citizen employment agencies devoted exclusively to finding jobs for older workers have sprung up. These services are expanding and generating more interest than ever before.

A senior citizen employment agency is usually established as a free community service, with no fee charged to the applicant or the employer. In many instances, the agencies are funded partially by government and partially by private philanthropic organizations. Their purpose and function is to attempt to match the prospective employee with a job, but often they extend other services to the applicant as well. They may provide counseling for their clients to help them adjust to the realities of the current job market. The applicant may be encouraged to express his feelings about aging and job rejection. Some counselors even practice job interview techniques with the prospective employee.

One of the most successful senior citizen employment agencies in the country is the Senior Personnel Employment Committee (SPEC) located in White Plains, New York. Since it began, SPEC has placed thousands of workers in numerous jobs. SPEC's motto is "Ability is Ageless."

One of SPEC's fastest growing innovations—it accounts for more than 35 percent of its job placements—is an operation called the Paid Neighbor. The service functions primarily in the field of home care. Paid Neighbors assist patients returning home from the hospital, take care of the sick and infirm, do light housekeeping, prepare meals, shop for food and other necessities, and provide companionship.

The Paid Neighbor service offers an excellent employment opportunity for the elderly individual who wishes to earn additional income but finds it difficult to compete in the open job market. A similar service begun by SPEC is the Paid Grandmother. Here elderly people work as babysitters on a steady basis for working parents.

SPEC has also designed a detailed outline on how to establish a senior citizen employment agency. This has been used by numerous new agencies in the United States, England, and Belgium.

The success behind many of the new senior citizen employment agencies may be partially attributed to the fact that these organizations try to capture the concern and involvement of the community at large. They stress that unemployment among the elderly is not just a governmental concern or a problem among the aged themselves; it's everyone's problem because everyone eventually grows old. These organizations stress that recycling older people back into the job market means a boost for the entire community because of money pumped back into the economy. Given the opportunity, older workers may indeed prove to be a valuable economic resource.

Another retirement option for the older individual whose need for additional funds is secondary to the need to be active is volunteer work. Nearly five million Americans currently work as volunteers. They provide services that are vital to many hospitals, clinics, and other institutions. The main advantage of volunteer work is that the worker can usually select the specific type of activity he or she wishes to engage in. Volunteers find places in hospitals, libraries, museums, courthouses, and political clubs, among countless other places. Some volunteers visit homebound people, tutor school children, or work in day care centers.

Retired physicians often waive their fee in free community health clinics; retired lawyers, accountants, and business people sometimes offer their services without charge as well. For the retired individual who is beginning to feel cut off from society, volunteer work may be the answer. The federal agency in charge of volunteer programs for older citizens is called Action. Its most widespread domestic activities program is called RSVP (Retired Service Volunteer Program).

We've looked at reitrement and retirement alternatives that are currently available in the United States. However, it is important to note that there are other innovative options for retirees being tried out in other countries. One alternative is known as gradual or phased retirement.

The idea behind phased retirement is that most people over sixty-five (and many between the ages of fifty-five and sixty-five) would be happy to earn less money in return for shorter hours, a lighter workload, and extended vacation time. These individuals would gradually phase themselves into retirement.

Sweden introduced its Partial Pension Scheme on a national scale in 1975. Under this system, a Swedish worker may switch from full-time employment to a part-time job and receive a partial pension along with a number of important company benefits. If he chooses to continue working part-time until he is seventy years of age, he will earn credits that increase his pension by the time he is ready for full retirement. The same worker can move toward eventual retirement gradually by each year lessening his work week by a few additional hours. The concept of gradual retirement seems tempting, but the Swedish endeavor is still too new to measure its success accurately.

Could phased retirement thrive in the United States? As yet no comparable scheme has been initiated, but some labor unions have pushed for gradual retirement options for their members in recent years. If these unions eventually achieve such demands, organized labor along with other groups will undoubtedly launch a serious campaign to make this alternative more widely available.

In the end, the way in which each person deals with retirement becomes a highly individualized matter. Although a pattern may be partially shaped by past experiences, the retiree may be required to develop a new attitude toward life. The years ahead can be a time to adapt a different lifestyle. Retirement doesn't have to be an ending, but a new beginning.

An Active Senior Center

A SENIOR CENTER is a facility dedicated to meeting the needs of older adults. It's actually a type of community center, often offering recreational, educational, and minimal health services for the elderly. The first senior center began in New York City in the 1940s and continues to operate today. Since the '40s the number of senior centers has greatly increased—there are more than five thousand such facilities actively operating in the United States today. A recent study has shown that at least one-third of the population over sixty-five has visited a senior center at some time. Some gerontologists believe that senior centers may reach more mature citizens than any other institution in America.

A close-up view of a typical senior center shows that most centers carry on a variety of activities simultaneously. A typical senior center is permanently housed and employs a staff of professionals who offer an ongoing program of services and activities. It may be housed in a store front, or a church basement; or it may operate out of its own designated building. Some centers serve about thirty people on a daily basis, while others are used by hundreds of visitors each day.

The type of people who come to a senior center help determine the individual character of that facility. The needs of the membership will determine what types of programs and services have priority. Whatever the differences among them, all senior centers help older adults fulfill their everyday needs comfortably and provide an assortment of varied activities to stimulate their interests.

A typical day at a senior center might include a morning poetry writing class, in which participants can evaluate and discuss each other's work and progress. During lunch time, a free hot meal would be offered in the cafeteria. Most of the free lunch programs sponsored by senior centers are paid for by the federal government. After lunch there is usually a special event such as a concert, a cosmetic demonstration, or, say, a lecture and demonstration of flower arrangement. For those who may not care to attend the major event, a dance class or a pottery workshop might be available.

The courses offered at a senior center are geared both to entertain and educate. A typical selection might include courses on opera appreciation, cooking, sewing, needlepoint, French, yoga, bowling, Ping-Pong, and chess. If a senior center is affiliated with a local college or university, its members may be invited to sit in on classes.

The following schedule of events demonstrates the average week at a typical senior center.

Monday, May 11th

Line Dancing with Rose	10:00–11:30 A.M.
Westchester County Mobile Unit (I.D.'s, Blood Pressure, Legal Aid, Energy Assistance Program)	11:00–2:00 P.M.

Tuesday, May 12th

"Shell Craft" lessons with Arlene Rogers	10:00–11:30 A.M.

Bingo with Seymour   1:00 P.M.

Wednesday, May 13th

Choral Group Session with Noel   10:00–11:00 A.M.
Hart

Special Guest—Joseph Curtis,   1:00 P.M.
New Rochelle Commissioner of
Human Services. Informative,
entertaining, delightful exer-
cise. Lecture directed for
Seniors.

Thursday, May 14th

Seed Painting with Arlene   1:00 P.M.

Friday, May 15th

Exercise for Health with Emily   10:30–11:30 A.M.

"Fix it" with Andy   12:45 P.M.

Bridge and Games with Lou   1:15 P.M.

The address below was presented by Katherine Studwell, Director of the Senior Citizen Center in Bronxville, New York, at an annual meeting of the Senior Citizen Coordinating Council. It provides an accurate picture of senior center activity.

In honor of Senior Citizen month, the Bronxville seniors were asked by Citibank if they would use the bulletin board space in the Pondfield branch for a display. The seniors in Bronxville have designed a bouquet of flowers to salute spring. There will be handmade flowers and in the center of each flower will be a picture of an activity the club has described on the stem. The whole bouquet will be tied together with a ribbon as our "Salute to Spring."

Since our flower sample says education, let's start here. The seniors in Bronxville have been taking French lessons for the past two years. A small group still meets on Thursday afternoons, while a larger group of people has been meeting on Friday mornings at the Reformed Church. They meet for refinement of conversational skills and are so far above me that I have been known to walk in, say "Bon Jour," smile broadly, and hopefully leave them with the impression that I can speak French.

We have another wonderful group of ladies and

gentlemen going over to the Office for the Aging each Friday morning to take part in a college-level course called Autobiography of the 20th Century. It is the hope of the Eastchester Historical Society that they will be able to use some of the stories written by senior adults for their permanent Westchester file. The bridge course, which has become so much a part of our senior center and has been so successfully run by volunteers over the years, is highly pleasurable education. The ladies and gentlemen who are taking the course are constantly calling upon their brain power to develop new techniques.

Perhaps the question most often asked by the members of our senior center is, "Can we do something for the needy?" The membership has always come up with a positive answer. During this past year we have been able to donate a rocking chair filled with books to the Westchester Day Care Center—all purchased with money we raised for this project. We were also able to make up table decorations for Meals on Wheels recipients for Valentine's Day. In addition, last Friday thirty-eight women gathered at the center to make chicken and rabbit hand puppets for brain-damaged children. We have also undertaken the job of dressing up all the dolls at the local day care center for Easter.

These group involvements have tremendous psychological value for the senior adult as they afford him a new sense of achievement. These projects offer a social situation with a purpose. In addition to craft activities, we are the fastest senior envelope stuffers in the county, completing seven thousand envelopes this spring for the Bronxville chapter of the American Red Cross.

Our physical fitness program offers our ladies and gentlemen an opportunity to keep their muscles and tendons limber and flexible. The Bronxville Senior Center also offers educational lectures on nutrition and other health matters. We sponsor free blood pressure clinics, while the senior citizen mobile unit from the county grants free legal services.

Our programs are varied and are in keeping with the interests of the group. They have ranged from slide presentations on travel to other countries . . . to lectures about the International Conference on Women and the Italian-American contribution to life in Westchester. There have been first-run movies, one-day trips ranging from a visit to the UN to a Christmas luncheon at Silvermine Tavern and a tour of the Gallery and Museum. We have had book reviews, theater parties, a fall vacation to see the foliage as well as a Christmas visit to Bethlehem, Pennsylvania. If ours sounds like a busy schedule, it is. Our center constantly tries to offer the elderly positive new references, abundant role models, and solid self-images.

Bronxville has one of the heaviest concentrations of elderly people in the county. By sheer numbers we are where the rest of the country will be at the turn of the century. In an effort to meet the needs of our community where such a large portion of the people are senior adults, we started a new senior information and referral service recently. As director of the Bronxville Senior Center, my goals are to try to seek solutions for unmet problems, to increase the coordination of existing services in the community, and to develop effective new outreach programs. As a resident of the village of Bronxville and Director of the Senior Citizen Center, my home phone is known and utilized a great deal.

Many of the requests for help come not only from senior adults themselves, but also from their families, neighbors, and friends. I have been able to assist seniors and acquaint them with a referral network of essential facilities which include homemakers, home nursing care, health education, and recreation. Questions about Medicare and social security benefits have got to go to the top of the list of the ten most important problems facing the senior adult. Often the elderly are faced with forms and programs which in actuality are quite incomprehensible. It is too often a confusing world for the aging American, and I am reminded of a poem I read recently:

I think that I shall never see
any form plain enough for me
a form that I will not detest
or take as more than painful jest.

A form with pages I can read
and fill out easily with speed
but forms weren't meant for fools like me
nor even God who made a tree.

So much of what we do at the center is supportive.
Every effort is being made to keep the senior adult
aware of what is available to him in the vicinity, and,
of course, every effort is being made to try to help the
older person remain in his own home. It's taken a bit
of time, but today the senior center is becoming better known and is being even more utilized than in
previous years.

It has been said that in America childhood is ro-
manticized; youth is idolized; middle age does the
work, wields the power, and pays bills; and old age
gets to sit in the rocking chair. Through the efforts of
our center many measures are being made to change
this image, to make senior adults continue to be a
vital contributing part of our lives.

Senior centers are important because they fill a
vital space in the lives of many older Americans. If

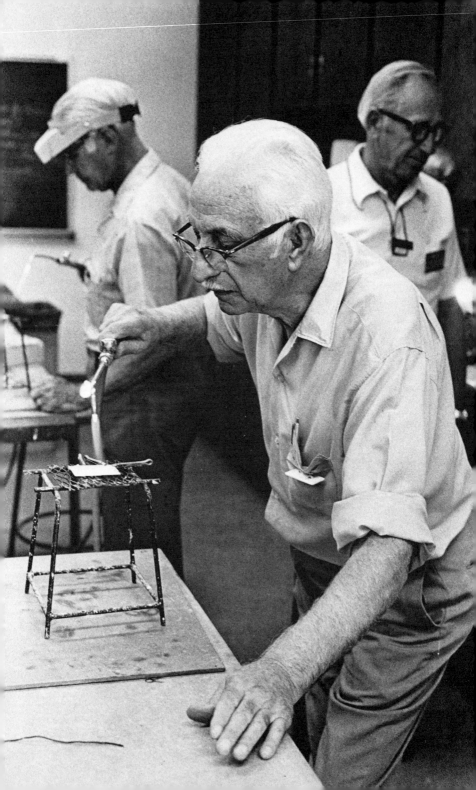

you are seventy-five years old and feeling alone and depressed on a rainy day, but are fortunate enough to live in an area in which there is a senior center, you can go over to the center, have a cup of tea, engage in some pleasant conversation, and be entertained by a movie or a lecture. Modern senior centers occupy an important place in the fight to combat social isolation among older Americans.

Adult
Communities
—A Way of Life

IN RECENT YEARS increasing numbers of older adults have chosen to live together in various adult communities of one sort or another. Perhaps one of the first types of communities to be inhabited primarily by mature individuals was the trailer park or camp. In the early 1950s, some parks were established primarily for people who had retired.

Trailer ownership increased as older adults came to enjoy the life of the parks as well as the housekeeping ease of a trailer. For the older person, the parks offered security and a peaceful existence.

Often a modern mobile home park is an attractive secluded community taking in an area as large as twenty or twenty-five acres, crisscrossed by streets and divided into small plots for the homes. It usually contains about two hundred mobile homes. People generally do not use their cars within the park area —they walk or bicycle instead—but each home has its own driveway; there is likely to be a lawn or patio area as well. The center of a modern, well-equipped mobile home park usually holds a recreation facility that offers a wide variety of activities for the residents.

From an economical point of view, a greater number of mature Americans looked to mobile home parks as a housing alternative. Once the trailer was paid for, the only additional cost to the retiree was the small monthly rental fee. An additional bonus was the fact that, unlike a house, no property tax is levied against a trailer.

In the 1950s, another commercial development began to attract the interest of senior citizens. Called an adult community or a retirement community, it was the creation of a small-to-medium-sized town especially designed for senior citizens.

Sun City in Phoenix, Arizona, was one of the earliest, well-publicized large communities of this type. It attracted national attention in the 1960s when it first appeared on the scene. A whole world in itself, it heralded thousands of other adult communities across the country in the next decade. A new trend was underway. Generally, residents of a retirement community do not have to be retired; they merely have to be past a certain age.

Adult communities are much more than a place of residence. They offer a whole new way of life. The homeowners, who may not feel inclined to be involved with the maintenance of their home or gardens, have the option of letting the management association take over this role.

The thrust of such an arrangement is to keep the residents happily and actively entertained. At a central location a community center will offer foreign language classes, disco dancing, yoga and exercise sessions, or perhaps workshops in pottery, photography, creative writing, music appreciation, and many other subjects. There is often a gymnasium, a sauna, a sewing room, Ping-Pong tables, tennis courts, indoor and outdoor swimming pools, and a lake equipped with boating facilities. Most adult communities provide local bus service to nearby shopping and recreational areas, too.

Perhaps the greatest attraction of adult communities is the tendency to draw middle-class people of similar interests and ages together. Many residents who felt isolated and cut off in their former city apartments now report that they've formed new friendship networks.

Romance often blooms at these adult communities, due perhaps to people constantly meeting in social situations. Bertha, a member of the welcoming committee at the Villages, an adult community near Freehold, New Jersey, met Joe, a recent widower, when he purchased a retirement home at the complex. As a member of the welcoming committee, it was Bertha's responsibility to make certain Joe was comfortably settled in his new quarters, had an opportunity to become acquainted with the area and his new neighbors, and was introduced to the activities the complex provided.

Bertha's and Joe's relationship began to grow. The couple found they had much in common, and the activities offered at their adult community provided an opportunity to embark on new ventures. Both had been table tennis players for years, but after only a few months of competition together, Joe and Bertha became the Ping-Pong champions. They took painting lessons, an art appreciation seminar, a course in conversational Italian, and signed up for a two-week senior citizen trip to Italy.

Joe and Bertha enjoyed one another's company so much that they found themselves spending most of their waking hours at one or the other's home. They decided that when two people want to be together to such an extent, the only sensible thing to do is marry—and that's what they did!

Their wedding was held in the recreational center of the complex. All of their friends attended, and the community's minister officiated at the ceremony. Bertha wore a beautiful wedding dress designed especially for her by the women in her sewing class. Her bridal bouquet was made up of flowers grown by the community's gardening club. After a reception at the recreation center, Joe and Bertha visited the homes of several close friends, where they sampled home-baked wedding cakes made by their neighbors for the occasion.

It is estimated that there are well over 600,000 mature adults living in adult communities in addition to approximately two million retirees living in mobile home parks. The desire of older Americans to live in communities designed especially for them is gaining support.

The homes in most mobile home parks and adult communities are bought by the individuals who live in them. There are, however, housing projects for mature adults that are government funded or sponsored by a social agency. Generally, to be eligible for such living quarters, the applicant's income must be below a certain level. Since the mid-1950s over 700,000 older Americans have lived in such housing projects.

The goal of these housing projects is to provide the older adult whose income may be near the poverty level, with decent living quarters. Although the occupants of such dwellings hardly have a luxurious lifestyle, the buildings are usually well maintained, have good security systems, and enable the residents to socialize readily.

Another concept that deals with meeting the housing needs of the elderly is congregate housing, which attempts to keep elderly people who are not totally self-sufficient out of nursing homes and other types of institutions. In congregate housing, groups of elderly people who are not well enough to live completely on their own live together in houses or apartment buildings. Such an arrangement tends to generate a sense of camaraderie among the residents. Typical of the services provided might be a cook, a cleaning person, and some minimal medical care. Sometimes the staff at a congregate housing center

might include a part-time activities therapist and a nutritionist. A college student may be hired to sleep in at night in the event of an emergency.

There are some who argue against any type of living arrangement in which older adults are isolated from people of other ages. They argue that a segregated residential situation tends to keep the mature adult cut off from the fabric of everyday life. In this respect, older Americans become excluded from the affairs of the rest of the community.

Most mature adults who live together in mobile home parks, adult communities, or congregate housing situations are doing so out of choice. Under certain circumstances, it can be extremely helpful to live near people who have shared similar experiences and who can offer advice as well as support. If growing older entails learning new modes of behavior, it might be easiest to do this among people who have already successfully encountered the obstacles in the development of a new lifestyle.

There are also some senior citizens who just enjoy being around people their own age. As one retired elementary school teacher residing at Sun City in Phoenix, Arizona, expressed it:

Now don't get me wrong, I love kids. I had four

children of my own and they've given me eleven grandchildren in all. I see my family on the holidays and I usually spend the summers visiting with one or another of my children. I also must admit that I fully enjoyed every year of my teaching experience. There's no other career I would have ever chosen. It was wonderful to watch young people grow and learn.

But there's also a lot to be said for the peace and quiet I enjoy now. In an adult community, you don't have to worry about getting your toes run over by a five-year-old tearing around on his tricycle, if you take a stroll down the street. You can sit in the park or in the community gardens without hearing little kids yell whose turn it is to go on the swing. Teenagers can be a lot of fun, but I don't care for rock music played at a blaring pitch at all hours of the night. And who needs to find beer cans strewn along your lawn the morning after one of their parties? At this point in my life I don't value excitement the way I once did. Now I want peaceful serenity, and I've finally found that here.

Statistics have borne out the fact that in recent years increasing numbers of older adults have become interested in banding together to form communities especially geared to their needs. This lifestyle is not right for everyone, but for some it has provided significant satisfactions, and it remains a viable alternative for elder Americans.

Successful Maturing—A Close-up View of How Some Individuals Handled Growing Old

SOME AMERICANS HAVE managed to turn their old age into inspiring success stories. These individuals did not achieve wealth or fame as a result of their aging, but rather gained a deep sense of personal satisfaction by sculpturing their experience of growing old into a time characterized by richness, variety, courage, and independence.

One such man is Allen Charles Bennett, who began his life on a farm in Illinois. As a boy, Allen spent a good deal of his time watching the government surveyors at work on nearby land. At times the workmen allowed the wide-eyed little boy to peer through their instruments or delighted him by letting him help put away their equipment.

When Allen wasn't watching the surveyors, he spent many of his after-school hours on the banks of the nearby Illinois River, peering at the infrequent shipping. Allen loved the farm, the river, and the bridges, so it was not surprising that he eventually graduated from the University of Illinois as a civil engineer. He was later employed by the federal government's Corps of Engineers, where he soon became an expert at surveying and mapmaking.

As an adult, Al Bennett was a rather quiet and shy individual. He had never married, and he spent most of his spare time engaged in hobbies like reading, photography, and freshwater fishing. At the age of fifty-eight, Al began to contemplate retiring before he turned sixty-five. He reasoned that his pension would come to about 40 percent of his salary. As Al had always been a frugal person, his savings combined with rental income from farmland would make it possible for him to leave his job. Once retired, Al would also be able to pick up odd jobs occasionally as a surveyor.

Al decided he wanted to retire and embark on a

new life. Within the first month of his retirement, he found that he was able to sell the small house he had owned. As he wanted to be free to travel, he decided to leave his accumulated possessions of forty-odd years behind. The only baggage he intended to carry was light clothing, cameras, fishing tackle, and his old surveying equipment. Blackie, his Labrador retriever, would accompany him.

Many locales seemed appealing to Al, but he wasn't sure where to go first.

Al felt that the area of his choice should have good scenery, good fishing, and perhaps other retired people with whom he could socialize. Al narrowed his choice to three states: Arizona, Florida, and Maine. In some respects, Al felt Maine was the most desirable. He knew he could afford to buy a cabin in the woods or even on the shore of a remote lake and enjoy beauty and solitude.

But ultimately Al concluded that he had already spent too much of his life alone. He longed for someone with whom he could share his experience. As a result, he spent a good deal of his time contemplating the possibility of marriage.

He imagined that meeting a suitable companion would be more difficult in rural Maine than in

Florida. Besides, Florida was noted for its fishing. So, armed with a new fishing reel and the hope of meeting someone special, Al journeyed south.

Al experienced some loneliness on his trip, but he resisted the temptation to write or call friends. Instead, he went over his priorities, his aims, and a new strategy for his retirement life. He wanted to make friends, marry if given the opportunity, maintain a strong financial position, and, most of all, preserve a happy outlook. He felt he could achieve all of these aims, but he was determined not to leave his life to chance. He intended to pursue actively each objective.

Once in Florida, Al bought a home. He spent the following few months making improvements on his new property and becoming acquainted with his neighbors. When everything was finally in order, he sat back and started to study the "business opportunity" section of the newspaper. With a small-to-moderate sum of money available, Al felt he could risk a business investment.

He was more interested in involving himself with a business activity than in turning a large profit. Therefore, he was free to look into unusual situations. One of them had to do with a tropical bird store which sold beautiful and expensive parrots and macaws, but generated few sales. The owner, a widow, needed additional capital. Al liked the owner and enjoyed handling the birds. He sensed correctly that the high price of the birds discouraged both teenagers and retired people from buying them. He suggested to the owner that he would become a partner in the enterprise, provided certain selling policies were changed. One of his ideas was that birds could be returned or exchanged within a specified period after purchase. Another suggestion was that the store offer to insure the birds on a yearly basis.

Before long, Ruth Costello and Allen Charles Bennett became partners in the Bird of Paradise Exotic Bird Shop. Al thoroughly enjoyed the hours that he spent working at the store. He was a good salesman and also built large bird cages that were offered for sale in the store.

Al found Ruth Costello a pleasure to work with as well as to spend time with socially. He admired her vivacious personality, good character, and logical thinking. After a time, Al didn't know whether he so looked forward to going to work because of the pet shop or because of his partner's presence. So it wasn't surprising that before Al had spent a full year in Orlando, he married Ruth. Since their marriage,

the couple have opened three additional pet shops in Florida. Their union can best be described as a truly growing partnership! And Al Bennett has accomplished what he was determined to do when he retired.

Sam Lazarro came to this country from Italy when he was six years old. His father died when he was eight, and as his stepmother was unable to care for her own children and Sam's two brothers and a sister, she placed the young boy in an orphanage.

At the age of fourteen, when children were permitted to work, Sam left the orphanage to live with his uncle. Once at his uncle's home, Sam soon obtained a job as a shipping clerk. He spent one year at this job. It was the only time in his life he would work for a salary.

While still on his first job, Sam spent his lunch hours going to dress factories where he would try to sell belts. It was a modest undertaking, but Sam became aware that he was a natural salesperson. He loved introducing himself to people.

After leaving the shipping clerk's job, he went into his uncle's restaurant supply business as a salesman, working on commission only. He worked for his uncle for nearly ten years. Then Sam tried to open his own business, but the timing was bad. The Depression was just starting and Sam's new venture failed. This was doubly disappointing, because his new wife was pregnant.

Sam was forced to return to selling for his uncle, but not for long. Several years later, Sam set out on his own once again. He began a one-man business; he would do the buying, selling, and shipping as well as keep the books. At last, Sam was a success! He found he had a propensity for attracting customers—people liked him, they felt he could talk their language.

Things were going very well for Sam when disaster struck. At the age of forty-two, Sam was found to have cancer. Early detection, surgery, and a fighting spirit saved him. With the aid of two employees, Sam ran his business from the hospital.

After his operation, Sam was somewhat handicapped, and he had to curtail his business activities. Nevertheless, he managed to put his son through college.

Before long, the age of sixty-five was staring Sam in the face. Sam was just as good a salesman as he ever was, and he was experienced.

Perhaps because he was a salesman without a fixed salary, Sam had never learned to save his money. In any case, as friends and relatives retired, Sam was forced to continue his business. If asked about it, he would explain frankly, "I can't afford to retire."

Now Sam is not as active as he once was. He sells his wares only one or two days a week.

Sam Lazarro spent his retirement years continuing to do what he had done all his life.

Money Matters

FINANCE IS ONE of the greatest concerns among the elderly in America today. Older people who are often forced to live on fixed incomes are daily faced with the dilemma of paying for food and shelter as well as medical expenses not covered by insurance. Older individuals who are no longer employed generally draw on one or more of the following sources for income: social security payments, pensions from former employment situations, personal saving accounts, investments in stocks and bonds, veteran's benefits, welfare payments, or assistance from children or other family members.

A closer examination of income for the elderly reveals that fewer Americans than is generally believed receive any kind of pension from their jobs. Only about 12 percent of the people over sixty-five years of age collect a pension from either public or private sources. Although many pensions from government jobs have a cost-of-living adjustment written into them, pensions granted by private companies generally do not and are therefore greatly diminished by inflation.

Another negative factor regarding private pension plans from private corporations is that very few offer survivor benefits. If a man works for a company for twenty years, builds up his pension, and then dies two years after retirement, his wife and children cannot collect any further monies, no matter how much of his salary was paid into the pension plan during the years he was actively employed by the company.

Perhaps the greatest flaw of private pension plans is that some never pay off at all. Unfortunately, due to financial irregularities that appear to be prevalent in many pension systems, a retired worker may never come to realize his rightful benefits after his retirement. Such injustices helped lead to the passage of the Employment Retirement Income Security Act (ERISA), whose major purpose is to promote pension reform.

Public pensions, which cover a number of federal, state, and municipal employees, often offer extremely generous retirement benefits. The future of such liberal pensions are currently in jeopardy, however, as it seems doubtful that many cities will continue to be able to offer its unions such generous allotments. The day of the enriched civil servant may soon be over.

Even today, the widows of federal employees may find themselves in more difficult straits than they had imagined they would be, as the survivor of a retiree receives only 50 percent of the retirement benefits slated for the deceased.

Often veterans, as well as their widows, over the age of sixty-five are eligible for a small monthly veteran's pension, if their incomes are sufficiently low to qualify for this benefit. Very poor elderly people may be able to obtain Supplemental Security Insurance (SSI), which will help provide them with some additional financial resources. Individuals who are self-employed are permitted special tax concessions while they are working to enable them to start a Keogh Plan that will later serve as a retirement fund.

Most of the elderly in America derive the majority of their income from social security. Social security was originally enacted by Congress in 1935. Its main purpose was to provide financial resources on a monthly basis for retired workers. The United States was not the first nation to develop a social security program. Over twenty-five countries had instituted benefits for retired workers before this country did, with Germany initiating its program more than fifty years prior to the American system.

According to the early German system, a worker could start collecting benefits at age sixty-five even if he continued his employment. Since in the late 1800s few people lived very far into old age, such benefits did not produce a drain on the economy.

When President Franklin D. Roosevelt introduced the concept of social security during the Depression as part of his New Deal program, its purpose was to force older workers out of the job market to make way for younger workers. As a result sixty-five became the mandatory retirement age.

The Social Security Act has been changed a number of times over the years in order to extend its coverage in various areas. Social security now also includes benefits for survivors, disability insurance, Medicare, and Medicaid health insurance programs. Individuals are also now allowed to retire at sixty-two and receive benefits, but at a 20 percent reduction rate. One out of every five people currently receiving social security benefits is not an older retired worker, but instead may be a disabled worker, a widow of any age, or a high school or college student whose parent is disabled or dead.

The social security system has always been financed by equal payments made by employers and employees. The amount of the retired worker's check depends on an average of the last years of his earnings when he was actively paying into the social security fund. Unlike other countries, the United States does not make contributions into the social security coffer from extraneous sources of tax revenue.

In recent years, however, a critical problem has come to the nation's attention—the social security system is undergoing a serious financial crisis. The problem can be simply stated: money is going out faster than it is coming in. On one end of the scale, retired workers are living longer and collecting more benefits than ever before, while conversely the declining birthrate and sometimes high unemployment statistics mean that there are fewer workers paying into the social security system to keep it running smoothly.

There have been numerous ways proposed to remedy this financial dilemma. Perhaps one of the most obvious solutions is to decrease the benefits being paid out currently or to at least keep them at their current level, disregarding any cost-of-living increases. Many people, however, regard this as a cruel, inhumane solution. Since the 1960s it has been shown that poverty among the elderly has been steadily rising. Today millions of Americans over sixty-five live below the nation's poverty level. Many of these individuals did not experience severe financial difficulties until they retired. With social security as their main source of income, it is difficult for these Americans to deal with inflation.

Another solution currently proposed by some to make the social security system solvent is to increase the payroll taxes of working people now paying into the system. Taxes of this sort tend to be inflationary, however, as they add to labor costs and subsequently these costs are reflected in higher prices. It also penalizes people who derive their income from salaries rather than from dividends or interest on stocks or bonds. In addition, there has been a backlash from many younger workers who are angered by the fact that they have less in their weekly paychecks because so much of their salary is being used to support an older generation.

Many workers have mistakenly believed that social security taxes taken out of their paychecks were being held in trust for them by the government until they retired from their jobs. In reality, the social security system is financed by each new generation of workers supporting the workers who have already retired.

Another proposal for lifting the social security system out of its fiscal difficulties is to take the money out of income tax revenue paid to the government by all citizens. The opposition to this solution stresses that since social security benefits are tied to wage earnings and the amount the retiree contributed from his accumulated salary, the paycheck should come solely from wages withheld for this purpose.

Other proposed remedies have included the initiation of a national sales tax of some sort or federal borrowing from the general treasury fund to remedy any deficits the social security system should incur.

Unfortunately, the fate of the social security system may be largely influenced by politics, special interest groups, and the mood of the times. People tend to have very different philosophies about how the aged in America should be supported. Some individuals firmly believe that social security must remain a wage-related system with each new wave of salary earners providing the benefits for those workers who have already retired. Others fiercely disagree and insist that the fate of the elderly is the responsibility of every American. They believe the financing of resources for the aged should come from government taxes.

As older Americans band together to form a political power block of their own, it's highly likely that some dramatic changes will take place. As early as 1978, Congress voted to extend mandatory retirement age from sixty-five to seventy. This means that many workers will be contributing to the social security trust for a longer time and will be collecting benefits for fewer years.

This alone will not save the system, however. An entirely new type of plan might have to be devised to help the elderly maintain a decent standard of living. Many individuals are in favor of a government-guaranteed income for every American over sixty-five. This would assure senior citizens, who have perhaps worked all their lives, that they will not be forced to spend their remaining years in poverty.

Even disregarding the threat of reduced benefits, many older Americans cannot adequately survive on their social security incomes, as the following cases show.

Maggie Ross is a frail ninety-six-year-old woman who lives alone in a small furnished room in New

Jersey. Her tiny quarters are hardly livable—the room is cluttered with old yellowed magazines and books, and piles of filthy clothing lie in two corners. The room has a dank smell, and swarms of cockroaches race along the stove and dishes and across the bathroom floor. For months Maggie has felt too weary to even begin tyring to clean it by herself, and she has no one to come to her aid. It takes a great deal of effort for her to even walk from her bed to a chair. Her only contacts with other human beings tend to be short and infrequent.

Maggie Ross's life wasn't always like this. At one time she had been the wife of a prominent New York businessman, and she had enjoyed many luxuries. When her husband died, Maggie believed that she would be able to live out her life comfortably on the money he had left her. Things did not turn out as she had expected, however.

When Maggie was about seventy-four, she was struck by several serious illnesses. This greatly dissipated her funds. In an effort to hire someone to take care of her and help her meet her daily needs, she was forced to sell her home. When the money derived from its sale was gone, Maggie was still quite sickly and practically destitute. She had outlived her own money. Her social security benefits are not enough to support her adequately. Today Maggie is old, alone, and living in poverty.

Edward Williams's story is another case in point. At eighty-one, Edward Williams was picked up by the police when he was reported by neighbors to be wandering aimlessly through the streets of Providence, Rhode Island. Upon being questioned by the police, Mr. Williams appeared confused, dazed, and even a bit frightened. At first, he was unable to remember his name, address, or where he was going.

The police drove him to the emergency room of a nearby hospital. After a thorough medical examination it was determined that he hadn't eaten for several days and the he was suffering from severe dehydration.

The man was immediately admitted to the hospital where he was given food and fluids. Within a short time he regained his memory, appeared coherent, and was once again able to function normally. He was then able to explain to the doctors that he had been forced to use his social security check to pay his rent, as his landlord had threatened to evict him if payment was not immediately forthcoming. Mr. Williams paid the rent bill, and then didn't have enough money left over for food.

People who have always been poor may remain poor into their old age. What many Americans do not realize, however, is that these poor people are joined by significant numbers of people who have *become* poor after growing old.

When social security payments become the sole or principal source of income, the elderly often have a difficult time. Today's elderly were brought up to value pride, self-reliance, and independence. In many instances they have struggled against adversity and won. A significant number of retired workers collecting social security benefits once believed in an American dream that promised a golden old age if they worked hard all their lives. For many of these people, the gold has tarnished.

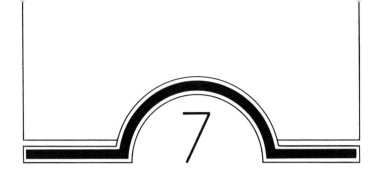

The Legal Side of the Aging Question

THROUGHOUT THE LAST fifty years a number of major pieces of legislation regarding the aged has been enacted by Congress. In addition to these federal laws, states often pass legislation that may affect the lives and welfare of the elderly in their own areas. For example, while Congress passed a law postponing the age of mandatory retirement from sixty-five to seventy, the state of California had its own legislation that prohibited forced retirement when the decision is based solely on age.

Perhaps the first piece of major legislation affecting the elderly was the Social Security Act of 1935. Social security provides a form of old-age insurance based on the retired worker's prior earnings and contributions to the social security trust. Although social security benefits are not sufficient to allow retired workers to live out the rest of their lives with financial ease, they have done much to combat extreme poverty among the aged.

Medicare is a government-sponsored system for financing health care for the aged. It was established in 1965. An individual becomes eligible for Medicare on his sixty-fifth birthday. He may go to any social security office to sign up for his benefits.

Medicare covers both hospital and medical insurance. Medicare's hospital insurance helps pay for the cost of the individual's hospital stay, certain specialized nursing home care, and a very limited amount of home health care services for a patient just returning from the hospital. Medicare's medical insurance helps pay the cost of office visits to doctors. Individuals enrolled in Medicare are required to pay a small monthly sum for the service. If they are admitted to a hospital, they must also pay for a portion of their hospital stay.

Medicare has dramatically altered health care for the aged in America. It has enabled literally thousands of elderly people who could not afford to help themselves but were in need of surgery and medical treatment to get the necessary care.

The Older Americans Act was also passed in 1965. This legislation was designed to set up a community-level network of services that would help permit the elderly to remain in their own homes. Under this act, federal grants were provided for the states to allow them to set up their own programs to aid the aged in such areas as housing, nutrition, health care, and transportation.

One very successful program that came about through the Older Americans Act is Project Assist. This provides aid to elderly crime victims in the Washington, D.C. vicinity. Over two hundred aged crime victims have received help from the agency in the form of emergency medical assistance, replacement of stolen funds, and a reimbursement for stolen food stamps. Project Assist has been used as a model in other areas to help elderly crime victims.

Congress has extended the Older Americans Act since its inception in 1965. In 1972, Title VII was passed to help improve nutrition among the elderly. A specialized food program was established whereby inexpensive hot meals were made available to the aged at local schools, churches, senior centers, and other convenient locations. An additional extension to the Older Americans Act was the Community Service Employment Program, which provided modest funds to be used for special projects that would give work for the aged.

In 1967, Congress passed the Age Discrimination in Employment Act. This served to "promote employment of persons based on ability rather than age and to prohibit arbitrary age discrimination in employment." The law was designed to prohibit the employer from firing or discriminating against older employees simply because of their age.

Congress created Supplemental Security Insurance (SSI) in 1974 to replace a number of state-sponsored programs previously used to aid poor people over the age of sixty-five. The system is financed through government funds and taxes, and individuals must prove their financial need in order to qualify.

The Employee Retirement Income Security Act (ERISA) was enacted by Congress in 1974 to help put an end to abuses involving employee pension plans. The act forced companies to disclose how their employees' pension funds were being managed. It also set up an Office of Employee Benefits Security under the jurisdiction of the Department of Labor to investigate employee complaints regarding pension rights.

ERISA also required companies offering pension plans to supply their employees with all relevant details regarding the plans. It mandated that private companies use advance funding or reserve funding for their employee pension plans to protect the employee in the event of business failure.

In addition, ERISA permitted individuals not covered by a pension plan to establish an individual retirement account—an IRA — in which the person may invest an untaxed percentage of his earnings to serve as retirement savings. The worker does not have to pay income taxes on the amount he contributes until after he has retired.

Congress established the National Institute of Aging (NIA) in 1974 as one of the branches of the National Institutes of Health. Its major purpose is to conduct studies on various aspects of the aging process and sponsor further education and research in the field of gerontology.

In addition to laws enacted by Congress, congressional legislation has also funded a number of volunteer programs that sometimes award small stipends to volunteers. For example, the Service Corps of Retired Executives (SCORE) uses mature businesspeople to provide free management advice and general business counseling to small businesses in need of such expertise.

In the Foster Grandparent Program, individuals

over sixty-five are matched up with abandoned or handicapped children in need of love and support. The Retired Senior Volunteer Program (RSVP) places senior citizens in service-oriented positions throughout communities. The RSVP workers help out in such places as libraries, hospitals, and day care centers.

As senior citizens join together to form their own political pressure groups, it's highly likely that further legislation beneficial to mature Americans will be enacted.

One of the largest, strongest, and most financially stable advocacy organizations for senior citizens in the nation is the American Association of Retired Persons (AARP). Anyone over fifty-five years of age may become a member. The organization services the elderly both through the services it offers and the causes for which it fights.

For example, AARP learned through a sampling of its membership that elderly people spend an average of 10 percent of their income on drugs. Some use nearly half of their money for this medical necessity. In response to this need, AARP began selling drugs, both prescription and over-the-counter, by mail at prices 40 percent below market level. It also opened its own cut-rate pharmacies for those who needed their medication immediately. AARP soon became a major force in the effort to allow generic substitution of drugs at a lower price and open-price advertising of drugs.

AARP provides a wide range of services through which its members can get help in their struggle against various bureaucratic institutions. It recruits and trains volunteers to provide free tax advice to elderly people. It also employs individuals who fully understand the intricate rules of such government programs as the social security system, Medicare, and food stamps. It tries to make certain that needy elderly people do not lose any benefits to which they are entitled.

AARP's national headquarters in Washington, D.C., runs a sizable consumer assistance center, and the organization's national office as well as its many local branches publish informative documents and offer courses in areas of special need to elderly people.

In addition, AARP also acts as a powerful political lobby for its membership in Washington, D.C., as well as in the various states. With a membership of over nine million people, the organization is capable of capturing the ears of our country's lawmakers. So far, AARP has fought for improvements in social se-

curity, Medicare, property tax exemptions for the elderly, controlled funeral costs, and an even more permissive estate tax.

The Gray Panthers is an extremely vibrant and effective activist group. Its primary goal is to improve the general quality of life for older Americans. The original Gray Panthers' statement of origin describes what they are all about:

> We did not select our name; the name selected us. It describes who we are: 1) We are older people in retirement; 2) We are aware of the revolutionary nature of our time; 3) Although we differ with the strategy and tactics of some militant groups in our society, we share with them many of the goals of human freedom, dignity, and self-development; 4) and we have a sense of humor.

The group's headquarters is in Philadelphia, Pennsylvania, but there are branches of the organization in over thirty towns, villages, and cities across the nation. The Gray Panthers accepts both old and young members. The organization is primarily a grass-roots operation in whatever location action is taken. So far, the Gray Panthers have devoted a good deal of energy to combating age discrimination in such areas as housing.

At an American Medical Association conference held in New York City, the Gray Panthers convened their own alternative medical convention in the same city at the same time which they entitled, "Do We Need A National Health Care Service?" They invited doctors, nurses, social workers, union representatives, and health care planners to attend. These parties listened attentively as the Gray Panthers addressed the issue of health care for the aged and put forth strategies for change.

In Portland, Oregon, the Gray Panthers conducted their own telephone survey of local pharmacists to test the effectiveness of a drug law passed by the Oregon state legislature. This law requires pharmacists to reveal whether there is a lower-priced generic equivalent to any given prescription drug. Over two-thirds of the more than one hundred pharmacists surveyed volunteered no such information. Since that time, the Gray Panthers have launched an extensive campaign to petition their state legislature to mandate that pharmacists provide their customers with such information verbally.

The Gray Panthers in Oregon also launched an extensive examination of nursing homes in the state. They made unannounced inspections of the facilities, checked the kitchens for cleanliness, as well as the nutritional value of the food served, evaluated the general quality of patient care, and checked on the availability of the staff. The Gray Panthers eventually reviewed their report with the state health department.

In Springfield, Massachusetts, the Gray Panthers have established a Pension Reform Committee to help workers who have left their jobs before they were fifty-five, or those who have been denied pensions by new employers because they are over fifty-five. These Gray Panthers have made themselves loudly heard at ERISA (Employment Retirement Income Security Act) conferences. They also have established a firm connection with the Pension Rights Center in Washington, D.C. Gray Panther pension reformers have compiled their own highly informative pension rights booklet which they have made widely available.

In recent years it has been especially difficult for retired people living on fixed incomes to keep up with rising utility costs. After many frustrating experiences trying to deal with large utility companies through the appropriate consumer channels, the Gray Panthers of Kansas City, Missouri, sponsored a public meeting. At this meeting over five hundred elderly consumers took turns speaking at a podium for over two hours, openly verbalizing their complaints. The events of the day received considerable media coverage.

Gray Panthers protesting the elderly's housing problem in Los Angeles, California, asked the mayor if he expected older Americans to live in tents. They followed up their query with a spectacular demonstration in which hundreds of protesters strategically pitched tents in the heart of downtown Los Angeles. The Gray Panther demonstration became a moving dramatization of the need for affordable housing for the elderly. The protesters were joined by delegations from numerous other senior citizen groups and tenant organizations.

The Gray Panthers were successful in getting free checking accounts for the elderly in Long Beach, California, and in Washington, D.C. In Rhode Island, they secured free public transportation passes for senior citizens during off hours.

These and other activities devised by various branches of the Gray Panthers—as well as by other senior citizen groups around the country—vividly demonstrate that older Americans may soon become a powerful organized force, one not to be taken lightly by our nation's lawmakers. As they are joined and reinforced by sympathizers of all ages, their quest for a decent life past the age of sixty-five may soon become a national aim.

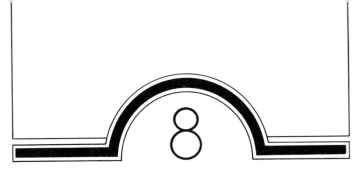

Growing Old—The Aging Process

IN OUR YOUTH-oriented society, many people are overly concerned with the prospect of growing old. As a result they have become preoccupied with trying to find ways to retard the inevitable process. The cosmetics industry has grown affluent by devising products that purportedly will ensure a youthful appearance throughout middle age and beyond.

Coping with the aging process, however, goes beyond vanity. People are often simply concerned with being able to live longer. Several theories have emerged in recent years that attempt to clarify what actually happens to people as they grow older.

One theory suggests that aging is controlled by a general timer or pacesetter centrally located at the base of the brain. Another speculation is that aging is not centrally regulated but instead is controlled by a biological timer in the nucleus of each cell of the body. A third theory purports that aging is the result of chemical changes of a hormonal nature within the nervous system. According to still another theory, aging is a breaking down of the human body's general immunity. Although one or perhaps a combination of these theories may be correct, the cause or causes of aging is still largely mystifying.

If research ultimately reveals the cause of aging and it becomes possible to retard the process, new and important questions would be raised. The effect of people living well over one hundred years of age on our social and economic structures would be disastrous. To date, a meaningful niche for people who are only in their seventies has not been found. How society would deal with a multitude of even older Americans would warrant serious consideration.

While some scientists are seeking to find a way to prolong life, others are addressing themselves to the challenge of producing a fully-functioning human being for a longer portion of his normal life span. Their goal is to create individuals who are healthy and productive rather than living out the final portions of their lives in sickness and misery.

Although some individuals refuse to admit that there are differences between the abilities of an old person and a young one, most scientists have acknowledged that there are certain changes in performance that come about primarily as a result of aging. Aging generally brings a diminished effectiveness in manual dexterity, as well as a slowing down of reaction time, the time it takes to respond to stimuli.

Some recent experiments with mice have shown parallel behavior to that of human beings. A dramatic reduction in learning ability by the mouse is usually a sure sign, despite a healthy appearance, that the animal has contracted a terminal illness. Death may occur in two or three days. When older human beings show a sudden substantial decline in I.Q., the drop in intellectual ability is an early sign of a serious health problem. The unfortunate person with such symptoms is likely to die within the next few years, or become so seriously ill that he can no longer be cared for at home. Researchers have found conclusively that a healthy human being will not experience a decline in general intelligence due merely to advanced age.

Although it is true that older individuals experience a slowdown in reaction time, their judgment and experience may more than compensate for this factor in on-the-job situations. Older executives and businessmen have developed methods and strategies which allow them to handle a tremendous amount of incoming data with speed and effectiveness. Thus, one cannot assume that they are less able to accomplish a given job just because they are older.

Until only recently, the government allocated very limited funds for research on aging. Perhaps this reality reflected our society's lack of concern for the fate of its older citizens. In the 1970s, however, a greater sense of awareness and responsibility arose. With the acknowledgment that a growing population of older people was a fact, several prestigious researchers turned to challenge numerous aspects of the aging process that are currently being explored. Perhaps the ultimate goal will be to lengthen and improve the quality of life for young and old alike.

9

Crisis— Medical Alternatives

A CRITICAL ILLNESS—it could strike any elderly person at any time. Such an individual may be living alone or existing on a low fixed income and be totally unprepared to deal with such an event. Heart disease is the leading killer among elderly people, followed by strokes.

Admission to a hospital for a critically ill elderly stroke victim can be as traumatic as the medical problem itself. Removed from the familiar, comfortable home situation, in some instances the patient may find himself in an environment of other critically ill patients. He'll be fed intravenously, perhaps surrounded by apparatus monitored by medical technicians who are too busy to talk or provide comfort and assurance.

If the patient is placed in an intensive care unit due to the severity of his problem, his family may only be allowed to be with him for about ten minutes out of every hour, leaving him to feel more isolated than ever. He may become so confused and anxiety-ridden that he might not even realize he is in a hospital. He is often not told the full nature and extent of his ailment, and thus may imagine the worst.

Once the stroke patient's condition has stabilized and he is no longer in a life-threatening situation, his family, along with the medical profession, may not quite know what to do with him. While his life would be best rebuilt by rehabilitation, too little emphasis may be placed on this alternative. More than likely, the patient will be transferred to a nursing home where he'll wear hospital garb, spend most of his waking hours in bed, and enjoy only limited opportunities for socializing. He may then come to envision the nursing home as a stopover before the cemetery.

For patients fortunate enough to be admitted to a modern rehabilitation center, however, their lives may be dramatically different. The Burke Rehabilitation Center in White Plains, New York, is such a place. Founded in 1915, it is one of the nation's largest such facilities, serving patients from the time they are discharged from a hospital to the day they are ready to return to their own homes and resume their former lives. Burke has both inpatient and outpatient facilities, and is associated with the Cornell Medical Community.

The atmosphere at Burke is warm and cheerful. Colorful pictures decorate the walls and inviting furniture is strategically placed in surroundings that are fresh, bright, and agreeable.

When the patient arrives at the center, the Burke staff assures him that he is not at a nursing home and that his chances of returning to his own home soon are extremely good. An effort is made to depart from some of the traditional hospital routines that may not be beneficial to the patient.

The patient is not forced to don dreary hospital garb; he is permitted to wear his own clothing. Whenever possible, he is taken out of bed and encouraged to sit in a chair. Since the problems faced by an individual entering a rehabilitation center may often be a mixture of physical, psychological, social, and economic elements, he is given an opportunity to consult with a psychologist, psychiatrist, social worker, and a chaplain in addition to numerous medical doctors. At Burke the staff attempts to involve the patient's family in his rehabilitation, too. The thinking is that a patient will be best motivated to help himself if he knows a strong support team is behind him.

Institutional routines are minimized at Burke in an attempt to lessen the patient's confusion. The focus of the therapy administered is to enable the patient to reenter society functioning at his fullest, despite his disability. The goal is to produce a vital, capable individual.

Life at Burke is designed to parallel life in the outside world as much as possible. Meals are served in the community dining area rather than in the patients' rooms, and patients are encouraged to walk, or, when necessary, move about the area in their wheelchairs.

After an average stay of two months at Burke, about 75 percent of the stroke victims are able to walk out of the facility totally unassisted, to return to their homes. It has been found that age is completely unrelated to ultimate recovery. The prognosis for a patient in his eighties is as favorable as for someone in his fifties. The tragedy lies in the reality that many elderly patients are never considered worthy of rehabilitation by medical professionals. Instead, they are immediately rejected because of their age and placed in nursing homes or other institutions.

Why *aren't* more elderly patients referred to re-habilitation centers after a critical illness? One reason is that our national health scene is geared primarily toward treating acute health problems. Services needed by people suffering from chronic disabling factors are considered secondary in importance. In addition, because rehabilitation is not included in most medical school curriculums, it is difficult to attract top physicians. Whatever the obstacles, one thing is certain: new services—ranging from re-habilitation centers to finding ways of helping older people maintain themselves in their own homes—must be developed to stop catastrophic illness from destroying the lives of mature victims.

One successful endeavor currently gaining ground throughout the country is the Shepherd's Center. The concept began in the summer of 1972 in Kansas, offering elderly people an alternative to institutional care by systematically providing home services and thus permitting them to remain in their own homes.

One important service the Shepherd's Center offers is the delivery of a hot noon meal. The meals are delivered by retirees who are still in good health, but who wish to help other people not as fortunate. Teams of six to eight people are assigned on a daily basis to deliver the food.

Another set of Shepherd workers known as the Transportation Volunteers use their own cars to take from twenty-five to thirty people a day to doctors' offices or to other facilities for medical treatment. The Visitation Program assigns volunteers to call and visit elderly people who live alone, feel isolated, and need to be reached out to. Still another program, known as the Handyman Project, utilizes the talents of over a dozen skilled people who make house calls to do minor repairs.

The Shepherd's Center's Crime Assistance Program trains volunteers who are over sixty-five to work with elderly crime victims. These volunteers provide safety instruction and prevention measures and help the victims deal with their own personal feelings of anxiety or anger. The Shepherd's Center has also instituted a Night Team, which staffs a twenty-four-hour answering service to help older people in the area who may find themselves in emergency situations.

The home services offered by the Shepherd's Center help keep elderly people out of institutions. The center also offers many additional services that do not center on home care. The Adventures in Learning Program offers courses and lectures on such subjects as history, speed reading, knitting, Bible study,

French, personal growth, gardening, and money matters. The Life Enrichment Program at the center brings together a limited number of older people who need additional love, support, and compassion. These individuals work together under the direction of an experienced professional to try to build up their emotional and spiritual resources. The center's noon-time program offers an outstanding speaker or workshop along with a nourishing, hot lunch. A desk at the Shepherd's Center staffed by volunteers offers discount coupons, a magazine exchange, and an opportunity to apply for a public library card and transportation passes.

Since personal health is a primary concern for many older people, the Shepherd's Center hosts its own annual Health Fair for people over sixty. About forty health agencies sponsor exhibits and screening tests, and offer lectures on general medical topics.

While advances in medical science have added years to the life span of humans, death still must be faced. A terminally ill patient cannot be left alone to care for himself. Yet there is little room for a dying patient in a typical hospital setting. Most hospitals are geared toward returning patients to society in good physical condition. Doctors, nurses, and other members of a hospital staff have been trained to cure sick people. They may feel a sense of personal frustration or loss when a patient they have been treating does not improve. Unfortunately, in many hospitals, much of the staff is not professionally prepared to deal with a dying patient and to help that individual come to grips with his fate.

In some hospitals, if a dying patient goes into a prolonged stupor, he will usually be moved to another room so that his presence will not upset the other patients. If the hospital has a room shortage, a folding screen may be placed around the bed. In effect, the patient is isolated from other people in the last days of his life.

Although most hospitals offer little in the way of support systems for the dying, the terminally ill, elderly patients usually have few other available choices. Some of the older adults will express a desire to die at home, but in many cases their families find it extremely difficult to care for them properly and comfortably.

Caring for a dying family member in the home can place a considerable strain on any family unit. The cost of medical care—not covered by insurance if the patient is at home—creates an enormous financial burden. In some families where all the adults work, a private nurse must be hired. Watching an elderly patient die at home can also create a tremendous emotional strain.

Taking all these factors into consideration, the question which arises is: Must all terminally ill patients who do not have families or whose families are not equipped to care for them at home die in impersonal hospitals? The answer is no. A new alternative is on the rise, and it is one many older adults are now looking to with great interest. *Hospice* is a medieval word that means a stopover station for travelers. There are now medical hospices where terminally ill people can go to die with personal dignity.

St. Christopher's Hospice in London, England, is a special kind of treatment center to which terminally ill patients can go to meet death as gently as possible. At St. Christopher's, doctors do not attempt to cure their patients; they recognize and accept the reality that these individuals are not going to recover. Extensive life-support machinery is never used. Patients are administered medication only for alleviating pain, anxiety, or depression. Everyone connected with a hospice has accepted the fact that fighting death by postponing it through mechanical means is less important to the patient than helping him prepare for it.

When a patient enters St. Christopher's Hospice,

he is met at the door by a nurse who personally welcomes him by name. After being escorted around the facility, he is taken to a bed that has already been prewarmed for him with hot water bottles. It is an important goal of the hospice to make certain that the patient is made to feel that he is never in anyone's way. All the staff members—not just those who are directly caring for the person—visit with the patient. This means that the office personnel, secretaries, elevator operators, and kitchen help all spend a portion of their day listening to the patients' expressed thoughts and feelings. To add to these resources, a large group of volunteers, often the relatives of former patients, work alongside the nurses.

The end result is a concerned hospice community vitally involved in providing aid to the dying. The hospice arrangement enables patients to enjoy family and friends, as well as as much activity as their physical condition may permit.

Helping the patient come to terms with his impending death is another important aspect of the hospice's therapy. Patients are encouraged to speak out about their feelings to relieve as much anxiety as possible. The staff continually makes a special effort to reassure the patient that he is not alone.

When St. Christopher's takes on a new patient, it

makes every attempt to work with the family. There are no stipulated visiting hours; visitors of any age and number are welcomed at all times. If they have the time, some family members choose to spend most of the day at the hospice, helping to wash and feed the patient.

One sixty-eight-year-old woman described what it was like to spend time with her dying husband at St. Christopher's.

It was just a few days after our thirty-fifth wedding anniversary when the doctors told me how pervasively my husband Henry's cancer had spread throughout his body. They informed me that unfortunately he now had only a few months left to live. It was so hard for me to hear and accept. I couldn't imagine what my life would be like without my husband, and I didn't know how I was going to cope with just passively standing by waiting for Henry to die.

My husband and I knew about the hospice movement. When we first learned about Henry's cancer, we had read all the literature on it in the event that the worst happened. Since we had been so close all the years of our marriage, we decided that we didn't want to be separated now, and we were glad when a few weeks later we learned that St. Christopher's would be able to accommodate us.

Henry's death turned out to be as peaceful as his life, and I am so glad that I was right at his side to comfort him as he passed on. He felt no pain. They always took care to be certain that he was provided with ample pain killers. I helped the nurses care for Henry, which lessened my frustration of feeling that there was nothing I could do for him any longer. The hospice's philosophy gave us more time together to try to learn to accept what was happening to my husband, and I'm grateful for the chance to have been able to share both my husband's life and death with him.

A large part of St. Christopher's function is to help the patient's family cope with losing a loved one. A dying patient who knows that concerned professionals will continue to help his family after his death may perhaps find it easier to accept that death.

The families of the patients come to know each other well at St. Christopher's Hospice. Visitors help one another through difficult periods, and in many instances a patient without a family will be cared for by another resident's relatives. A special club made up of the patients' family members meets monthly with the staff. There they can freely discuss their feelings in an atmosphere where they know they'll be accepted.

The trend towards hospice care for the dying is beginning to emerge in the United States. There are now well over fifty hospices throughout the country. Recently an organization called the National Hospice Association was initiated. Hospice supporters stress that a society that annually spends millions of dollars on pre-school playgrounds and national parks ought to provide its elderly citizens with a dignified place where they can go to die.

The Good Old Days

IN OUR THINKING there is a tendency to romanticize what old age was like for people in the past. We imagine that older people were given more respect, enjoyed more security, and generally led happier lives. Today's lower status of the elderly is blamed on modernization and the social forces that shaped America into a fast-paced, highly competitive industrial nation.

But was life really better for the elderly in the past? Have they fared better in other countries? Research discloses that in underdeveloped societies, where life was carried on in small communities, the aged were generally treated with respect and care. Contrary to what one might expect, however, such preferential treatment did not arise out of a sense of love, duty, or obligation. The elderly gained their authority and prestige because it was believed that they controlled the group's resources in one way or another. Underlying the high regard was some enforcing power to ensure it. In short, respect for old age was generally accorded on the basis of some particular asset the elderly possessed.

The two major resources often supposed to be held by the elderly were either wealth or some type of magical power. The younger generations therefore permitted the aged a certain amount of control. Among the Pomo Indians, a tribe in Northern California, children were taught to show courtesy and respect to the elders of the tribe, since the old people knew the most about poisoning. The same coercive respect was given to an aging father by his sons and nephews who hoped to inherit his property upon his death. Although such factors played a large part in shaping how the old were treated in preindustrialized societies, other more individualized factors helped to shape the manner in which they were related to as well.

Studies of the treatment of the aged in several agricultural villages in India reveal that elderly males, in particular, commanded a high degree of esteem.

According to village tradition, the oldest male was the head of the household. His wife served as his connection to the rest of the family. She delivered various orders or messages to other family members, particularly daughters-in-law and grandchildren, and transmitted any response back to her husband. In short, she acted as her husband's courier to several generations of family members under his authority.

The system succeeded well for the father unless his wife died. Under such circumstances, the daughter-in-law who was the oldest son's wife took over the courier role. Until then she would have had little or no contact with her father-in-law, the ruling patriarch. In many instances her new role left her emotionally torn between loyalty to her husband and duty to his father when authority conflicted.

Under such pressures, the eldest son gradually began to assume the authority and prestige accorded to his widowed father. As the older man's power eroded, he was reduced in status to being just another dependent member of the household. The new family dynamics diminished his role and with it the former value he held for his family. In line with the village's standards he should have received unlimited honor and respect, but in reality, he didn't receive any.

The situation became even more humiliating if the ruling male died before his wife, as her authority and prestige within the family stemmed entirely from her husband. Her own worth and accorded respect were buried with her husband. The eldest son rose to become the head of the family, and his wife took over her mother-in-law's role. The old woman was then completely dependent on her family's kindness, but too often she became the victim of the daughter-in-law who held what was once her own power. Again, though traditional respect for the aged mother might have been outwardly endorsed, her actual treatment in day-to-day life provided little comfort.

While the unhappiness and displacement of old people is too often laid on industrialization, family pressures may be equally to blame for a negative effect on the lives of the aged. At no time have families been completely harmonious units, with each member totally attuned and responsive to the others in his family grouping. Family tensions can become further strained when there is an abrupt transfer of authority from one member to another. Many of the problems the elderly are faced with today are not modern concoctions; such obstacles have existed for as long as there have been families.

Old age, even in a relatively simple communal society, is not a standardized fixed experience. It is a blend of the chance occurrences of life, the individual's own resourcefulness, and the combination of strengths and deficiencies inherent in each person's personality. Varying characters tend to shape different eventualities, even under similar circumstances. The satisfaction one may derive in his old age is the result of a blend of social forces, family life, and individual choices and reactions.

An extended family is one encompassing several generations which reaches out to include relatives other than parents and children. The young and the old of three or four different generations may live together in a single household and continually interact with each other on all levels. The old are considered a permanent part of the family until their death. Many people generally assume that the advance of industrialization put an end to the extended family and replaced it with the nuclear family. The nuclear family is comprised of only two generations: parents living with their children. It is often thought that industrialization broke up family clusters, severing the old from the support network of their loved ones and thereby leaving them to fend for themselves.

Research indicates that in the United States the

extended family network never really existed for the majority of people, however. Even in preindustrialized America, fewer than 20 percent of married people over the age of sixty-five lived with their married children. When their children married, they usually left home to establish their own residences with their new spouses, while their parents remained behind in their old homes. Things came about very much the same as they occur today.

It may be surprising to learn that older widowed people did not usually live with their married children, either. The majority of elderly widowed people lived in various places as boarders or resided in institutions. About 39 percent lived alone. Only a very small number lived with relatives of any sort.

It is interesting to note how the elderly have fared in other countries. In Japan, a nation that has achieved a high degree of industrialization, the aged still remain a highly valued and active segment of society. Perhaps it is significant that a great number of Japanese people continue to work well into their old age. Almost twice as many elderly people are employed in Japan as in comparative countries, and the reason is not always economic necessity. A majority of the aged Japanese who continue to work declare they do so out of a sense of duty, to remain active in order to maintain their health, or for the personal fulfillment they derive from their jobs. Family relationships involving older adults in Japan differ dramatically from prevalent lifestyles in the United States. For example, more than 75 percent of the population over sixty-five live with their children. The typical Japanese household comprises three generations: the aging parents, their married children, and their grandchildren. The Japanese family remains a tightly knit unit containing valued and respected space for the elders. This fundamental right of the aged to receive such general respect from younger people is an integral part of Japanese society's values, and it is also a basis for the ancestor worship that is a part of the country's fundamental religion and culture.

In Israel, a relatively new country, treatment of the elderly differs greatly. Part of planning a new society in Israel involved the development of kibbutzum, self-contained collective communal settlements throughout the countryside. The nature of an equalized group living/working situation, characteristic of such a collective, should have done much to dispose of the common problems usually faced by the aged who are out of the mainstream of society.

In a kibbutz, aging members could enjoy full economic security and on-site medical services. Retirement from work duties is gradual, and in any case the elderly are never cut off from the center of community life. Members are expected to remain in the kibbutz founded by their parents. In this way the aged may maintain a close and continuous relationship with their own children. Ideally, in a kibbutz, the elderly should be spared much of the isolation, inactivity, and subordinate dependency associated with aging.

Surprisingly, however, many individuals who have grown old in Israeli kibbutzim have not been as comfortable as might be expected. The explanation is ironic. The collectives, which helped the new nation develop and maintain itself during its early years of struggle, were founded on ideals of hard work, continual productivity, and self-denial. Life in a kibbutz means relentless physical labor balanced by spiritual rewards and a sense of belonging and unity.

Everyone in a kibbutz is expected to do his share and then some. These goals and objectives are an inherent part of every kibbutz member's philosophy, regardless of age. Therefore, when someone is advised to slow down, take it easy, or do less, he may feel that he would be betraying his deepest and most important commitment and belief. This shift is an extremely difficult transition for the elderly, who often experience a painful uneasiness as they grow older in such communal living situations.

Elderly kibbutz members also often feel an uncomfortable sense of dependency when they are forced to rely directly on younger kibbutz members for support. If an elderly person receives a state pension or a social security check, he is dependent on an anonymous government sponsorship, rather than on the people he must live with on a day-to-day basis. Although every effort is made to assure the older kibbutz member that he is entitled to this rest period in his life, he may feel somewhat inadequate about not doing as much as he had done in previous years.

Until relatively recent years, the aged faced a dismal future in France. Among many of the working class it was considered a far more fortunate fate to die while still employed than to face endless years of loneliness and financial hardship. Nineteenth-century medical research in France held the view that old age was unrelieved deterioration. At that time little was done for the elderly by the medical profession, inasmuch as it was believed that advanced aging was the beginning of the end, and consequently it didn't matter very much.

Things may be changing, however, as French seniors of the twentieth century set about carving out a better existence for themselves. In the past, there was almost total disinterest among French unions on the matter of establishing pensions for their retired workers. Yet in recent years, the union members themselves have begun to press for firmer commitments to pension resources and a choice of retirement options.

The French are also moving away from the concept that aging is a period of deterioration and wastefulness. In recent times there has been a dramatic increase in the number of marriages and remarriages among people over sixty-five. It is as though they are beginning to appreciate that old age can still be a vital, fulfilling period.

The life of an elderly person is greatly affected by a complex mixture of elements such as social environment, the family, personal resources, general health, and varying value systems. No single aspect can guarantee a joyous future for any aged individual, although an improvement in any of these areas may enhance that life to some degree. Improve any of these elements, and you improve old age for the individual involved. Old age need not be a time of helplessness and inactivity. The daily existence of older adults will improve when they use their own resources to effect changes in their options and channel their energy into creating better alternatives for themselves.

Old Age—A Time To Grow

OLD AGE DOES not have to mean an end to the exuberance and vitality of life. It doesn't mean that spiritual, emotional, or intellectual growth need come to a close. On the contrary, since older people often have more leisure time than people who are involved with their jobs or with raising families, they are likely candidates for new, unusual, expansive undertakings.

Today at least one out of every five colleges or universities in the country offers courses and programs calculated to meet the needs of older people. Institutions of higher education first took this step due to the declining enrollments of young students and because of federal grants available to academic centers that were willing to move in this direction. Such courses are not constrained by the pressures of grades, tests, and requirements. In these classrooms for the aged, something very special is going on—learning for the sake of knowledge.

The professors involved in these programs make the point that old people are not necessarily played out and untouchable, but are reduced to such a state through sheer neglect. They feel that these older students need new outlets for their many skills and talents as well as an opportunity to feel useful.

A number of full-fledged programs for the elderly are already in existence. One of the earliest was the Institute for Retired Professionals (IRP) at the New School for Social and Scientific Research in New York City. A number of years ago it began employing a unique "do-it-yourself" approach. The Institute, which is unusual in its elite enrollees, consists of retired doctors, lawyers, schoolteachers, professors, executives, and businessmen, who are busy creating their own educational and social community. At the Institute each student has the opportunity to both learn and teach, as all offered courses are conducted by members with no outside teachers involved. Among the courses offered have been French, Creative Dramatics, Music, Fiction Writing, and Recent

Medical Developments of Interest to Everyone. Class discussions usually reveal wit, humor, and insight, and sociability is clearly a valued dimension among classmates. In addition, the students from the Institute are also permitted to take courses in the outside school's brimming adult program. Many of them have found that they spend most of their weekdays on campus attending a variety of workshops and seminars as well as lunching in the school's cafeteria. The Institute may not be the answer for all retired people, but it has worked well for many older professionals. The concept of the IRP has served as an inspiration for the creation of other similar centers in Boston, Philadelphia, San Francisco, and Cleveland.

Many colleges and universities offer free or reduced tuition for senior citizens taking courses in their regular curriculum. Some innovative institutions have offered courses for older adults in such areas as preretirement planning, educational vacations, and even retraining for new career skills. North Hennepin Community College in Brooklyn Park, a suburb of Minneapolis, initiated an experimental tuition-free program for senior citizens which featured such practical courses as Budgeting on A Fixed Income, Lip Reading, Psychology of Change, Public Speaking, and preparation for passing the high-school equivalency examinations. Many of these older students later move on into credit courses and degree programs.

The Institute of Study for Older Adults believes in going where the students are, and as a result holds classes in retirement homes and at senior centers. The courses offered are suggested by the various groups in each of the centers where the students meet. At the close of each term of study, a "graduation" ceremony is given. For some of the enrollees it is the first graduation of their life, and many are not hesitant to note how thrilled they are about being awarded a diploma. Devising a suitable curriculum for these students is not an easy task.

Some of the students are illiterate or haven't completed grade school, while others hold advanced degrees from respected universities. In addition, while all these students refer to themselves as older adults, they range in age from fifty-five to over one hundred. Still, in spite of such obstacles, the program has been tremendously successful. Most of the teachers believe that the lack of structure, examinations, grades, and compulsory attendance results in a true learning experience.

One group of students that had completed a course managed to convince a local radio station to schedule a monthly spot on the air as a forum for issues relating to older Americans. Other students claim they have become revitalized and are channeling their new energies into working on various volunteer programs designed to aid senior citizens in various important aspects of their lives.

Programs on and off campus in higher education for senior citizens are likely to increase over the coming decades, as the elderly population and its needs grow. They may well become the newest and most vital frontiers of service for colleges and universities in the years to come.

Other types of personal growth experiences are opening up for older adults as well. Senior Actualization and Growth Exploration (SAGE) has brought the human potential movement to the field of gerontology through the creation of new programs especially designed for the elderly. SAGE began as the creation of psychologist Gay Luce, who firmly believes that the joyous experiences of life need not end after middle age. She used her knowledge to develop a series of workshops that encouraged older people to enjoy meditation, relaxation, and biofeedback techniques to feel better physically and mentally.

SAGE views old age as a time for opening new possibilities and heightening one's awareness of body and mind. Luce initiated a pilot program based on the philosophy that individuals can progress at seventy-five as much as at twenty-five if given the necessary conditions of support, challenge, freedom, and continual activity. To participate in her initial program the older individual needed a general willingness and openness to accept new concepts, an ability to perform the exercises (each person needed written permission from his physician to join the group), and a promise to practice what had been learned.

The SAGE methods are offered as aids to growth. No one is ever forced to do anything he doesn't feel comfortable with. SAGE expects each participant to grow in a different way, to find new possibilities for himself. The breakthrough to heightened awareness differs for each individual.

What SAGE actually offers is a path to an improved mental outlook that helps people see that they are capable of changing their lives, unlocking themselves, and sharing their experiences with others. When SAGE workers operate out of a nursing home, the residents eagerly await the visits, looking forward to meeting with them so that they may share their feelings. These are the same people who would otherwise spend most of their day sleeping. As one

eighty-seven-year-old woman explained to a SAGE worker, "Others bring music, crafts, and entertainment here. But you are the only people who allow us a time to talk and express what is really going on inside of us."

Epilogue

SO MANY UNPLEASANT assertions have been made about growing old that the material for this book grew out of an effort to balance the scale. Old age is nothing more than a period of our lives. It need not be considered more or less desirable than youth. It derives its value from the attributes society attaches to it.

Mature adults have the same capacity for growth, understanding, challenge, and humanity as any other age group. It is important to recognize and acknowledge the potential that is inherent in maturity, since everyone eventually moves to the same position that older Americans are in today. Many of our senior citizens have already risen above the prevalent negative stereotypes to carve out rich, fulfilling lives for themselves. But there are also others, unfortunately, who have been scorned and neglected; they have lost the confidence necessary to demand respect and a rightful place in our society.

By viewing older Americans as individuals who exhibit the various positives and negatives common to all people, we will free them from the very stereotypes which restrict their lives. It's an important goal, because none of us can be really free until that happens.

Bibliography

Bengston, Vern L. *The Sociology of Aging*. Indianapolis: Bobbs-Merrill Co., 1973.

Byerts, Thomas O. *The Environmental Context of Aging*. New York: Garland Publishers, 1979.

Cole, Ann P. *Yesterday's Children*. New York: Vantage Press, 1979.

Decker, David. *Social Gerontology: An Introduction To the Dynamics of Aging*. Boston: Little, Brown & Co., 1980.

Fry, Christine L., ed. *Aging in Culture and Society: Comparative Viewpoints and Strategies*. New York: Praeger Publishers, 1979.

Gelfand, Donald. *Aging: The Ethnic Factor*. Boston: Little, Brown & Co., 1982.

Lancaster, Helen. *Aging*. Independence: Herald House, 1980.

Langone, John. *Long Life: What We Know and Are Learning About the Aging Process*. Boston: Little, Brown & Co., 1978.

Rockstein, Morris and Sussman, Marvin. *Biology of Aging*. Belmont, CA: Wadsworth Publications, 1979.

Watson, Wilbur. *Stress and Old Age*. New Brunswick, NJ: Transaction Books, 1980.

Index

142

About the Author

Elaine Landau received her B.A. degree from New York University and her Master's degree in Library and Information Science from Pratt Institute. She worked on the editorial staff of a children's book publishing company and as a youth services librarian before becoming the director of the Tuckahoe Public Library in Tuckahoe, New York. She is currently the Adult Group Work Specialist for The New York Public Library.